TELL ME A RIDDLE

TELL ME A

RID

DLE

Edited by Dana Bruce
Illustrated by Frank Elkin

PLATT & MUNK, *Publishers*
NEW YORK

TELL ME A RIDDLE

What's the difference between here and there? The letter 'T'.

What passes before the sun without making a shadow? The wind.

Where should a billsticker sleep? In a fourposter.

You can have a room full of it but you can't have a spoonful of it. What is it? Smoke.

What runs without feet? Water.

Why is an old car like a baby?

Because it never goes anywhere without a rattle.

Why is a cello like a cashier in a bank?

It gives out notes.

Why is the lettuce the friendliest vegetable?

It's all heart.

Three men dug a hole in six days. How long did it take them to dig half a hole?

You can't dig half a hole.

How do you get down off an elephant?

You don't get down off an elephant; you get down off a duck.

Why is a mouse like clover?

Because the cattle eat it.

What is it that you can keep even
when you give it?   Your word.

What color is the newspaper when
you have finished reading it?

Red.

What goes up a ladder on its head?

The nail in a shoe.

What should a flock of birds avoid
flying into?   A rage.

Why does time fly so fast?

So many people are trying to kill it.

What is everyone doing at the same time?

Growing older.

What's the principal part of a horse?

The mane part.

At what table do you never sit to eat?

The multiplication table.

Where was the family when the fuse blew?

In the dark.

PLUNK

PLUNK

PLUNK

What color is a drop of water?

Pink, pink, pink!

When is your heart like a policeman?

When it keeps a regular beat.

Why are cowards like butter?

They run before fire.

How many sides does a coconut have?

Two, inside and outside.

Why do Uncle Charlie's slippers last
so long?   He never wears them out.

Why are many people like umbrellas?

They have their ups and downs.

Why should you never swim on an
empty stomach?

It's easier to swim in water.

What's always behind time?

The back of a clock.

Why is a clock like a condemned man?

Its hours are numbered.

When is a horse never hungry?

When it has a bit in its mouth.

Why is it rude to whisper?

Because it's not aloud.

Where did Benjamin Franklin go on his fourth birthday?

Into his fifth year.

What bar opens but never shuts?

A crowbar.

Why will you never starve in the desert?

Because of the sandwiches there.

What did the dromedary say?

I have a hunch.

When will the letter G surprise a farmer? When it changes OATS to GOATS.

When does A make a straight line crooked? When it makes ZiG-ZaG.

What word contains 26 letters? Alphabet.

What tongue never gossips?

The tongue of your shoe.

What's an eavesdrop-
per? An icicle.

What pine has the sharp-
est needles?

A porcupine.

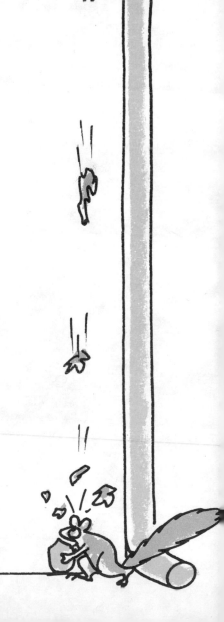

What's the best way to
keep dried prunes?

Don't return them.

Why does a dog wag his
tail?

Because no one else will wag
it for him.

When is a house no longer
a house?

When it's ablaze.

What's the difference between the North and South Pole?

All the difference in the world.

What's the best thing for hives?

Bees.

What does a horse say to oats?

Neigh.

What bolt will you never find on a door?

A thunderbolt.

Why was the rock emotional?

Because it was easily moved.

Why was the mackerel shocked?

He met the electric eel.

Why was the butter bad?

When it was cream it wasn't whipped enough.

When is a tooth like a plot of land?

When it's an acre.

What did the monkey say as he laid
his tail on the railroad tracks?

It won't be long now.

What is a twack?

A twack is what a twain wuns on.

What makes more noise
than a trombone?

Two trombones.

What do you take
when it rains?

Shelter.

What would a dolphin
at the kitchen sink
look like?

A fish out of water.

What sort of hawk is not a bird of prey?   A tomahawk.

What cap is never worn on the head?   A knee cap.

What does the barber find the easiest thing to part with?   A comb.

What wig covers the head but is never worn?   A wigwam.

What fruit grows on
telegraph poles?

Electric currents.

Why is a pack of cards
like a garden shed?

There are spades in it.

What pipes are never smoked?

Bagpipes and hornpipes.

Why did the dishonest man keep his word?

No one would take it.

What's the worst weather
for rats and mice?

When it's raining cats and dogs.

When is an elephant heav-
ier than an elephant?

When it's led.

When is a business letter
sharp? When it is filed.

What usually has more than two feet?

A skating rink.

What never uses its teeth to eat?

A comb.

What is nearer to you than to me, but I can see it and you can't?

The back of your head.

What's the difference between a watchmaker and a prison warden?

One sells watches and the other watches cells.

Where is generosity always to be found?

In the dictionary.

Why did little Timmy not mention his sore tooth after his visit to the dentist?

It went right out of his head.

Which has more legs, a kangaroo or no kangaroo?

A kangaroo has two legs; no kangaroo has three.

A kangaroo hops in front of two kangaroos, a kangaroo hops behind two kangaroos and a kangaroo hops between two kangaroos. How many kangaroos are there?

Three.

Why did the dressmaker want to avoid the crowd?

She thought she would be hemmed in.

When is a boat not a boat?

When it's a-shore.

Why is a nobleman like a book?

He has a title.

Why is a hat like a king?

It has a crown.

What letter does the shoemaker use?

The last.

What's the difference between a potato and a soldier?

One shoots from the eyes and the other from the shoulder.

Why is the letter D like a wedding ring?

WE can't be WED without it.

When is a boy like an orange?

When he looks round.

How do you make a window blind?

Fill it up with bricks and mortar.

Which candles burn longer, the candles in a birthday cake or those in a candlestick?

They all burn shorter.

What room is never lived in?

A mushroom.

What grows outward but never upward?

Ripples made by a stone
thrown in a pond.

Why are handcuffs like souvenirs?

They're made for two wrists.

Why is a gun like a jury?

It goes off when discharged.

What cane helps you move much faster?

A hurricane.

What did the sugar say to the spoon?

Don't stir!

How many potatoes can you put into an empty sack?

One. After that the sack will no longer be empty.

What's the difference between a high mountain and a spoonful of castor oil?

One is hard to get up and the other is hard to get down.

What did George Washington do with his boots
when he wore them out? He wore them home again.

Why is the word LILIES like a face?
There are two i's in it.

When is a clock angry?
When it strikes one.

On what side of the house
does a cherry tree grow?
On the outside.

Where would you find an elephant?

It's not easy to lose one, it's so big.

When do elephants have eight feet?

When there are two of them.

What luggage would you find in the jungle?

Elephant trunks.

Why is thunder like an onion?

It comes peal on peal.

What does a duck have that no other bird has?

Ducklings.

Who invented the steam engine?

Watts-his-name.

What country are children happiest in?

Lapland.

What goes from New York to Boston without moving? Railroad tracks.

What goes down deep and never can be dragged up again? A well.

What did the onion say when it was boiled in the stew? I'm not as strong as I used to be.

What's the price of the moon? Four quarters.

What color is the North wind? Blew.

What tune makes everyone happy? Fortune.

When a cat falls into the river, what's the first thing it does?   Gets wet.

What cats are always found underground?

Catacombs.

Why does a cat look at one side of the room and then the other when entering a room?

Because she can't look at both sides at the same time.

What has forks but never uses them to eat?

A river.

Why are soldiers and dentists alike?

They both have to drill.

Why do boys and girls buy licorice?

They can't get it for nothing.

How many sides does a golf ball have?

Two; inside and outside.

Why should secrets not be told in gardens?

Because of the beanstalk there.

What always has an eye open but can't see with it?

A needle.

What has only one foot?

A leg.

What is bought by the yard and worn by the feet?

A carpet.

What flower is very fierce?

A tiger-lily.

What key won't fit in the lock?

A donkey.

Why do people who write books look
so strange?   Tales come out of their heads.

What bell never rings?   A dumbbell.

When is a thief lazy?

When he takes things easy.

What kind of robbery is not danger-
ous?

A safe robbery.

How did the Admiral know there
wasn't a man in the moon?

He'd been to sea.

What coat never has sleeves or buttonholes?

A coat of paint.

How did the pig build a place to live?

It tied a knot in its tail and
called it a pig's tie.

What's the latest thing in
dresses?

Night dresses.

What has two thumbs and no
fingers?

A pair of mittens.

Why does the heron stand on one leg?

To rest the other one.

If you shoot at two birds
on a fence and hit one,
how many will be left?

None. The other one will fly away.

When can you carry water in a sieve?

When it's frozen.

Why is a watch like a river?

It doesn't run long without winding.

What has no feet but always wears out shoes?

A pavement.

What does a person have but can't hold for ten minutes?

His breath.

Why is the letter A like 12 o'clock?

It's always in the middle of day.

What would the landlady do if her tenant tore the curtain?

Put it down as rent.

What ants are the largest?

Giants.

What ant lives in a house?

An occupant.

What does a ship weigh before moving?

Its anchor.

What is smaller than an insect's
mouth?

What the insect eats.

Why do hens always lay in the day-time? Because they're roosters at night.

What chef in the kitchen wears the largest hat? The one with the largest head.

Why is a black hen cleverer than a white one? A black hen can lay a white egg but a white hen can't lay a black egg.

What did one goldfish say to the other
as they swam in the bowl?

See you around.

What is never out of sight?

The letter 'S'.

What is never part of anything?

The whole.

What grows shorter as it lives longer?

A candle.

What is of most use when it is used up?

An umbrella.

Why is ice cream like a race horse?

The more you lick it, the
the faster it goes.

When is a horse no longer a horse?

When he turns into a field.

What pierces and leaves no hole?

Sound.

Why did the man not go back to his
tailor?
He got a stitch in his side
after his first visit.

Why does a coat get larger when
taken out of a small suitcase?
You find it increases.

What turns without stirring?
Milk.

What did the new suitcase say to the
old one? You're a sad case!

What has no beginning and no end but has a center?

A circle.

How do you make a lemon drop?

Let it fall.

What letters are never tired?

N.R.G.

What's most like half a pumpkin?

The other half.

Why is a rooster a
very particular bird?

He won't lend anyone his
comb.

When is an elegant lady like a slice
of bread?

When she's toasted.

What has arms and legs but no head?

A chair.

When are the baker's hands like a garden? When they are in flour.

What pies will you never find in a baker's oven? Magpies.

What's the best thing to put into cakes? Your teeth.

Why did the elephant lie down?

Because he couldn't lie up.

Why is the inside of a cave so mysterious?

We can't make it out.

What is hard to beat?

A drum with a hole in it.

What do bees do to earn a living?

They cell their honey.

Why is the letter E like an island?

It's in the middle of the sea.

When do you spell best?

When you are asked to.

What changes a pear into a pearl?

The letter 'L'.

What people are the strongest?

Shoplifters.

Why is a canal a good place to keep money?

Because there are banks on both sides and locks every so often.

What scales can't be used for weighing?

The scales you play on the piano.

What's the proper diet for a dancer? **A few capers.**

What should a singer take before singing? **A deep breath.**

Why is the letter K a happy letter? **It's always in luck.**

What friends should you have around when you feel tired? **Only nodding acquaintances.**

Why did the llama look over the fence?

Because he couldn't look
through it.